Windmills

Written by
Jill Atkins

Ransom

Windmills have sails.

Look at some of the odd sails you might see on a windmill.

Gusts of wind turn the sails.

The sails turn cogs in the windmill.

Cogs are terrific tools. See how they all connect up in the windmill.

Then they all turn as one big tool.

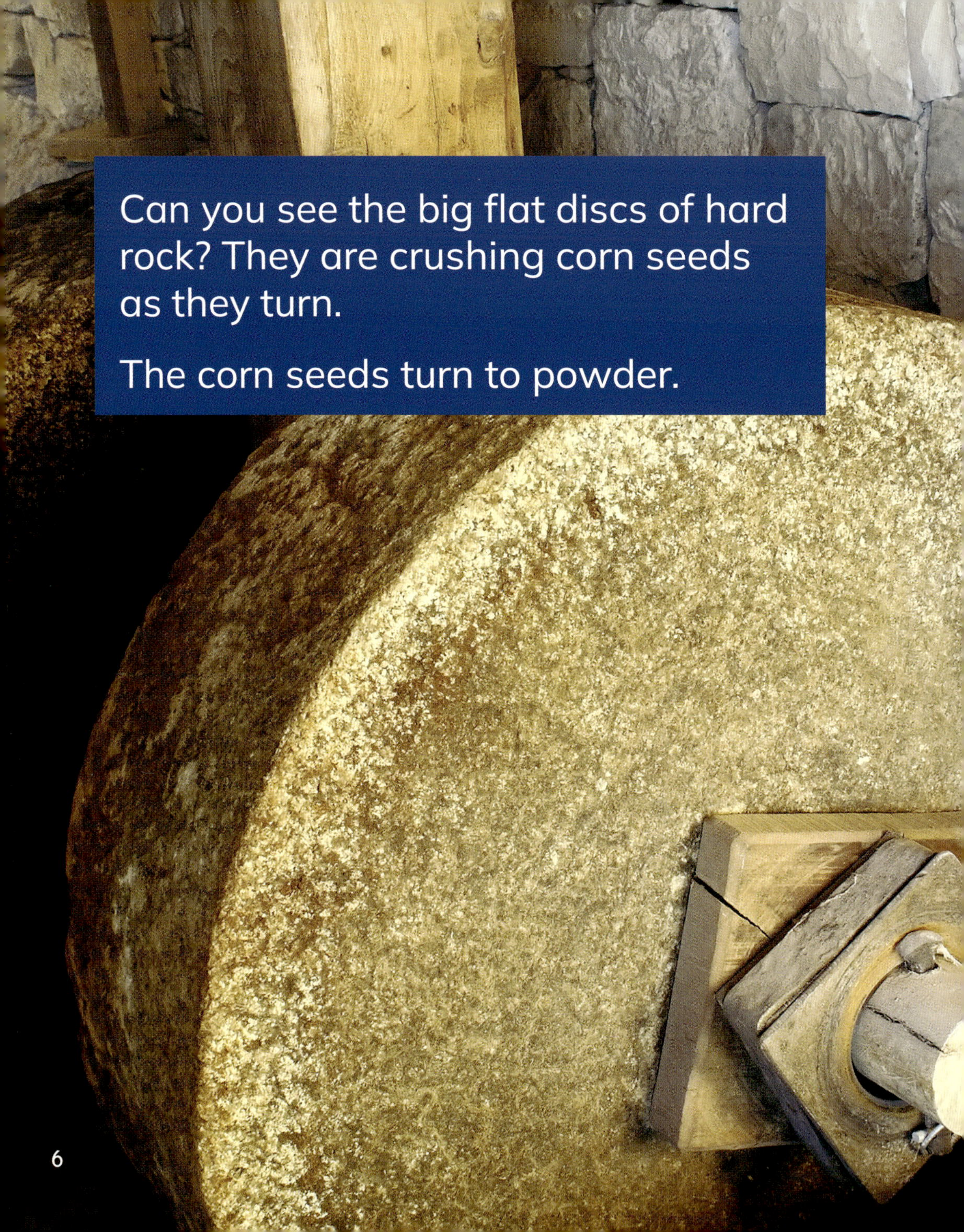

Can you see the big flat discs of hard rock? They are crushing corn seeds as they turn.

The corn seeds turn to powder.

The miller fills sacks with the powder from the corn seeds.

Then the miller sells the sacks for cooking.

This is not a windmill, but it is still a mill.

It has cogs too, but it needs a gushing river to turn the cogs.

Its discs crush the corn seeds, just like in the windmill.

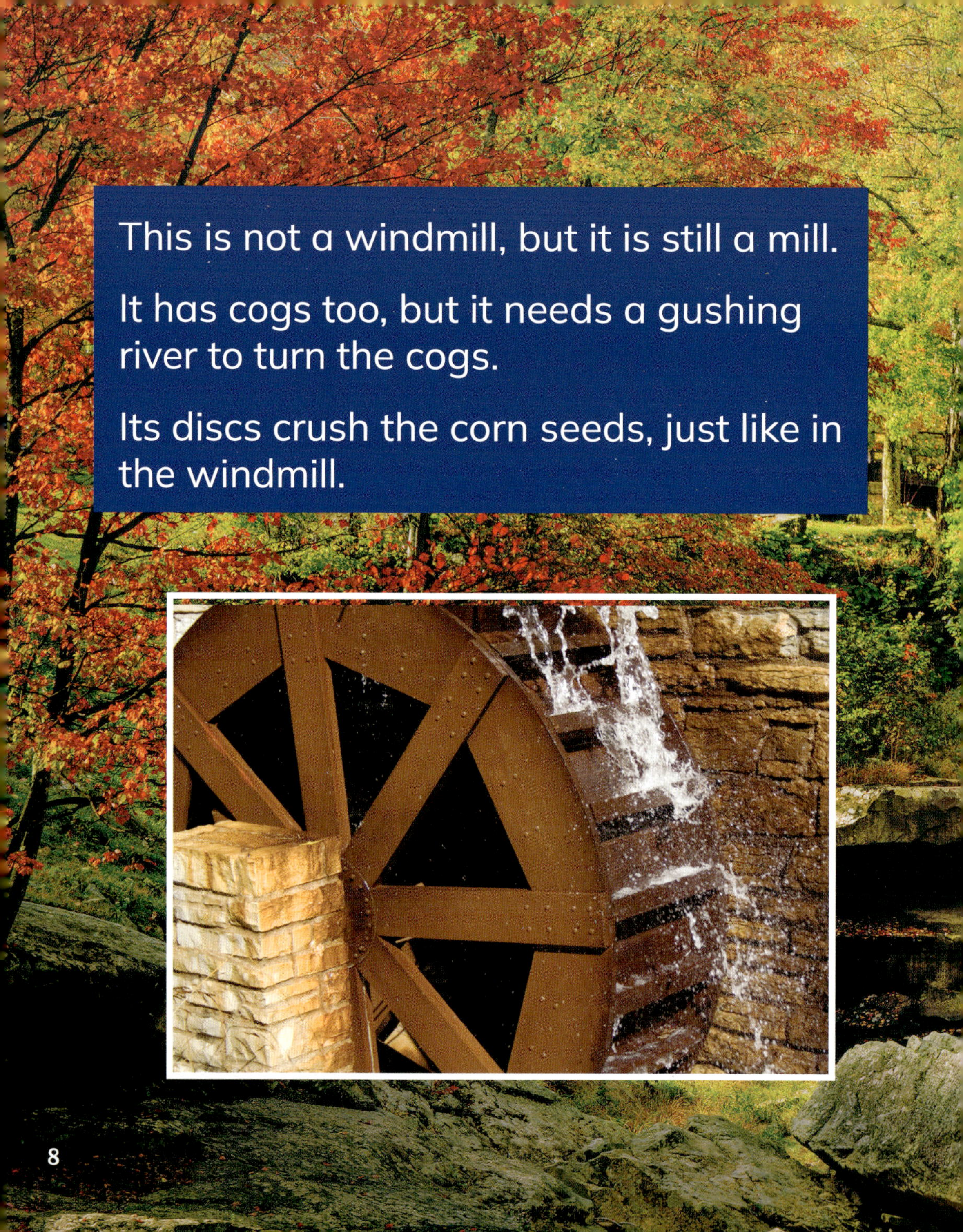

Some windmills pump liquid
out from flat land.

Some windmills pump liquid up from deep down under the soil.

This is good for the sheep and the crops.

This is a wind farm.

You might see hundreds of windmills.

Some are inland. Some are off the coast.

This is a big windmill!

We get power from this sort of windmill.

We get light from that power – and we can cook with it too.

We need windmills!